MW01051510

Dear One

by Emily Karlichek

Illustrated by
Casandra Bentley
Reggie Buchanan
Marissa Fowlkes
Heather Gonda
Nick Love
Aimee Sanchez

Edited by
Steph Cosmas

Graphic Design by
Mark Karlichek

Published by Createspace.

ISBN-13: 978-1548201005 (CreateSpace-Assigned)
ISBN-10: 1548201006

To my Dear One, Killian Markus.

You are my greatest adventure.

Another long day has come to an end.

Come into my arms, Dear One.

Let the fire within you burn to a smolder. I am here to ease you into the peace of night.

As I look down upon your face, I am called back to the first moment I saw you; then and now, I see you. All at once.

These moments are nothing but you, beautiful and content.

I study every detail, building an image to cherish forever.

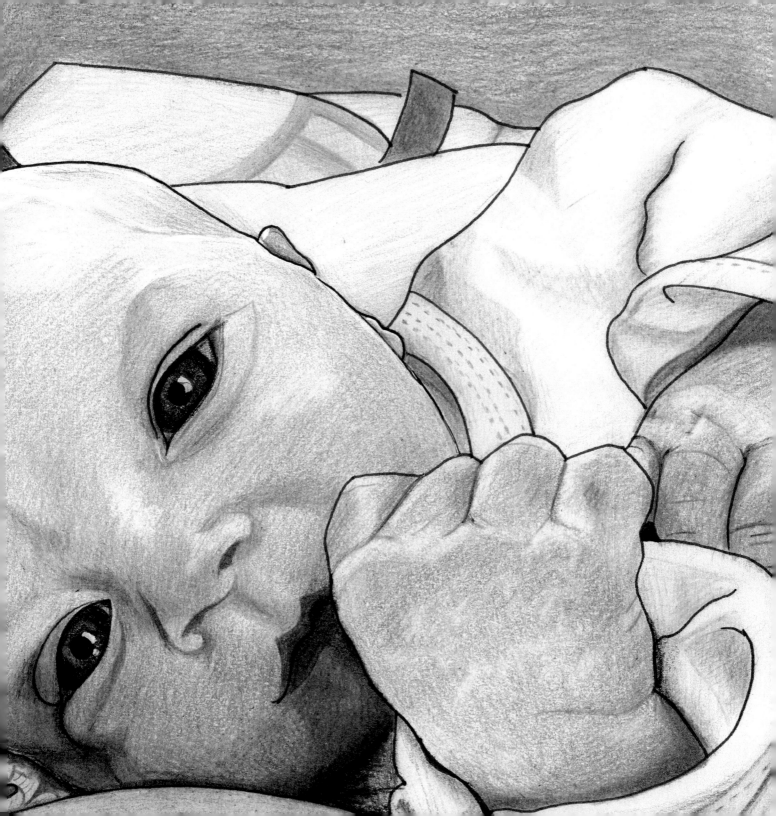

I kiss your forehead.

It is a whisper of the purest love into
the great wilderness of your mind.

I release my energy with this touch,
sparking the first fire on the edge of
the dark wild, where you will draw your
guiding light. You will carry me along into
the darkness; do not be afraid. Choose the
direction and speed of your exploration;
I will help light your way.

I will keep you safe - but I will keep you
moving toward the exciting unknown.

I smell your head, drinking in its unique
scent. As my cheek caresses your hair,
I am filled with gratitude for each perfect
strand, your creativity, your kind heart,
your electric spirit.

My child, you give me life - more vibrant,
fuller than I imagined was possible - even
in my wildest, most vivid dreams of you.

Your eyes are closed, your lids shielding you from the wonders and worries of the world, holding tight to your own dreams.

With a breath, your eyes flutter. You look at me. I am flooded with joy each time you awaken in a gaze locked with mine.

I was here all the while.
I never left.
I never will.

Hush now, Dear One. All is well.

Down the slope of your nose, I run
my finger, feeling the buzzing of your
thoughts. I kiss the perfect spot where
your nose begins, right between your eyes.
You breathe deeply, relaxed and content.

Just as we share our days - the warmth
of the sunshine and the cool of the
breeze - we share the same happiness.

Together, we are safe and protected.

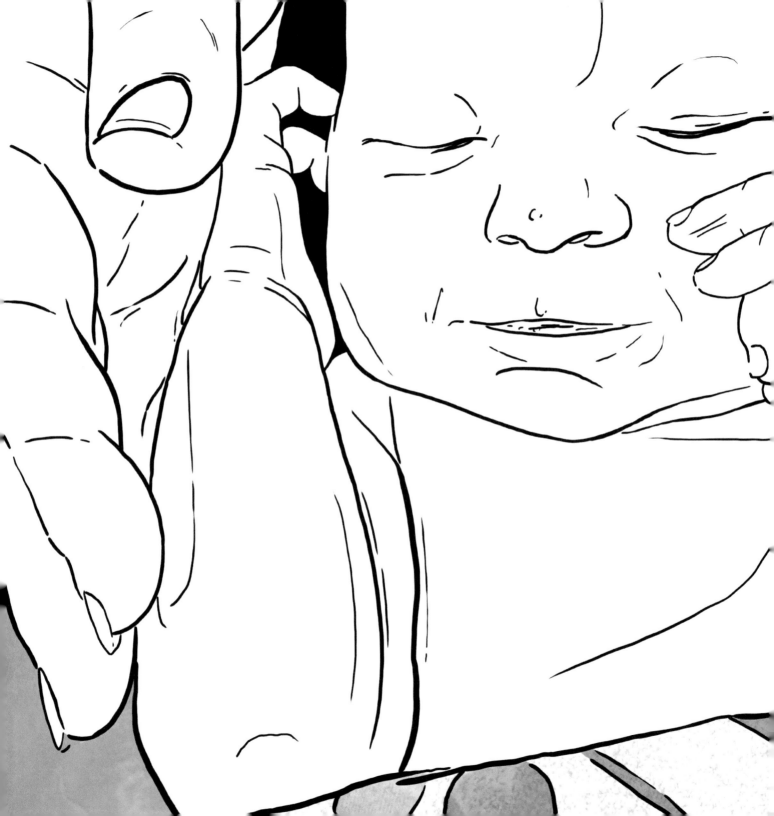

The curve of your lips recalls the power of your words and the gate which separates thought and sound. I try to feed your body and mind with the good of the earth, so with those lips, you may return beauty and love to the world.

I accept every sweet kiss you offer, knowing someday those kisses may not be given in abundance. You will grow up, and they will be a honeyed memory.

I wrap my arms around you, struggling to balance my need to hold you close and my charge to help you fly. In this life, no matter where you go, I will be waiting with these arms open wide to welcome you back to me.

I envelop you to protect you, to surround you with love.

I envelop you to protect myself from the heartache of your absence. Just one more minute, one more second, my love.

Just one moment to hold you before you grow one inch.

Wrestling in my own mind, I am ignited by you. Selfishly, I want you to stay little, who you are today. I am excited for what is to come, yet sad when moments quickly flutter away. Beautiful moments too fragile to hold, like a butterfly. Too perfect to be caged, yet so difficult to release into the big world.

My Dear One, my butterfly… Mine to protect, mine to set free; all your own to fly as the wind may take you.

Your head on my chest, my heart beats
strong and soft. As you drift further into
your dreams, do you hear my heart beating
through my bones to reach you? To fill
your ears with the tempo of my adoration?
To set your spirit's beat to the tune of
mine, at least for now?

No, my darling. You have your own beat,
in rhythm with mine, but not the same.
You are unique. Profoundly your own. The
song of our hearts is in harmony, but your
song is yours alone, meant to touch this
world just once in all of space and time.

My eyes move from your face to your hands, tucked warmly just under your chin.

I roll your little knuckles gently between my fingers.

What wonders these hands will create. Already, you paint and stack and throw and catch. You caress my face and say you love me. You show me your accomplishments and your frustrations.

Your hands are small but capable. They have already wiped my tears, as mine have wiped yours. But mine are weathered. Yours are fresh, soft, delicate... full of potential, and so strong. You will do mighty things for this world, for yourself and in the lives of others, in the days to come.

Your sweet face captures me once more. Your sleepy eyes focus on mine, and you breathe softly, sighing as you settle into deep, peaceful sleep.

My Dear One, I am so in love with your whole being: who you have been every moment until this one; who you are right now; who you will become. Love was defined when first I saw you, when first I knew you were mine.

Go courageously into the unknown.

Protect your heart, but do not hide it.

Care for your body, but challenge it.

Expand your mind, but do not poison it.

Follow your heart to find your joy.

Give your joy to the world.

You, my Dear One, are my
greatest adventure.

I will always be here loving you...
wherever your adventures may lead.

Casandra Bentley is a graphic designer, illustrator, food lover, and thrift store fashion maven. She studied both graphic and fashion design at Kendall College of Art and Design of Ferris State University. Casandra lives life to the fullest with her two daughters and loving husband.
Email: casandrabentleysm@gmail.com

Reggie Buchanan has been on an artistic journey since he moved to Los Angeles in 2009. Coming from Florida, he had aspirations of becoming a professional hip hop dancer. He had opportunities to be in commercials, music videos, a tour and Shake It Up on Disney! In the last 3 and a half years, Reggie has been studying Media Arts and Animation and just recently received his Bachelor's of Science. The journey continues and to keep up with his work, follow him on IG @reggiebuchanan.

Marissa Fowlkes was raised in East Michigan and has deep roots in the Tennessee mountains. Focusing on a happy middle ground, she is working towards a degree in material science and fine arts, and gains inspiration from the in-between of reality and imagination. She explores and tries to connect with all life around her, learning from everything. She uses knowledge and time to build a colorful future with her family. Instagram: marissalynn_art

Heather Gonda is a senior Psychology major at Western Michigan University. She has always loved art. She paints and draws when it feels right, mainly focusing on human portraits, though cats have recently become a fun muse.
Instagram: retnicole

Nick Love grew up in Empire, MI and moved to the Twin Cities for school where he attended the College of Visual Arts on Summit Avenue. He enjoys video games, his dog Bailey and lime popsicles.
www.45thstudios.com
Instagram: 45th_studios
Fortyfifthstudios@gmail.com

 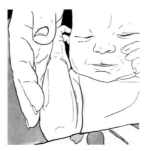 

Aimee Sanchez graduated from Baylor University with a Bachelor of Fine Arts degree. She gathers ideas for art projects by taking regular trips to the beach with her husband and two sons. Surfing in the summer and drinking hot tea in the fall are two of her favorite things.
www.thebelovedsea.com
Instagram: @thebelovedsea
Facebook: Aimee Sanchez Art

Steph Cosmas is a freelance editor, proofreader and self-proclaimed bibliophile uprooted to the Midwest all the way from Austin, TX where she attended The University of Texas, studying Sociology and Italian. She is extremely proud of her Greek heritage and is madly in love with her little family: husband Kevin, cat Clancy and dog -- best bud -- Wyatt. Steph lives for travel and nature, and her favorite night of the week includes a softball game with pals.
Instagram & Twitter: @StephCosmas
Website: StephCosmas.com

Mark Karlichek is an automotive industry professional, loving husband and father by day, and a freelance graphic designer by night. He earned a Bachelor of Fine Arts degree from Western Michigan University with an emphasis in graphic design. Currently he works in the automotive world and enjoys hobbies like wrenching on cars, painting miniatures and spending time with his wife and son.
Instagram & Twitter: xDetroitMetalx

Born in Holland, Michigan, Emily Karlichek has lived and traveled across the US and in 2012 she settled in the Metro Detroit area with her husband Mark. In 2014 they welcomed their son Killian Markus, who is her muse and was the inspiration for her first book, "Dear One."

"Dear One" began as a love letter to Emily's son, written on scraps of paper and in various journals. In writing about the joy and the bittersweet nature of watching the child she loves growing, Emily found a feeling most parents and caregivers can relate to - watching with excitement as the little dear ones in their lives grow, while yearning for time to slow down. As Emily continues to watch her son grow and change, she has kept mental snapshots, physical notes and journal entries about all the things she wanted to tell him, her hopes for him, about all she felt as his mother. This book is a simple story with an emotionally complex yet universal message for anyone who has cared for a small child. Emily has lived as a mother with big dreams and hopes for her son's future, while holding tight to each precious moment before it passes and he grows any older. This internal battle is fought and felt by parents, grandparents, caregivers and adults of all kinds who have a special child in their life. This book is a monument to loving a small child with all your heart - and feeling every part of that journey.

This project was very unique in the exercise of collaboration with many talented artists; Emily chose photographs of her family, and asked six different artists to each produce several illustrations for the book. This mix of artwork added several key elements to the book that Emily felt were very important: variety of artistic mediums and styles, diversity of artists who bring different backgrounds to the project, and an opportunity to show families of different compositions. Emily wrote the book with universal themes, keeping parents and caregivers of all kinds in mind. It was crucial to her to bring a diversity of perspectives to the project through the visual telling of her story.

A graduate of Western Michigan University with a Bachelor of Arts in public history and English, Emily is thrilled to be following her dream of becoming a published author. Her full time career is in nonprofit development and leadership, and in her spare time enjoys writing, crafting, and exploring all that life has to offer with her family and friends.

Thank You for making this book possible through your support of the Dear One Kickstarter Project.

Alma Sobo	Heather Dixon	Matthew, Candace &	The Renda Family
Amanda Conrad	Helen, Lauren & Jim	Lincoln Perales	The Romanosky Family -
Amy Palarchio	Jack Warners	Megan Carolin	In memory of our
Andrew Hamilton	Jacob Love	Megan Ricica Kennedy	Dear One, Deanna
Ashley Gatesy	Jason Lareau	Michael G. Apple	The Stears-Macauley Family
Ashley Guillen	Jeni Piechocki	Mom & Dad	The Sulak Family
Ashley Martin &	Jesse Cwalina	Mrs. Wisdom Harris	The Switlik Family
Joel Squitieri	Jessica Patterson	Nathalie Demers	Tina Janel Barnett
Brad Rudich	Jim & Nanette Watkins	Nick Atkins	Tommy Proulx
Brooke Adams	John Cooley	Nick Vanden Huevel &	Vikki Hardy Brown
Bruce & Margie Johnson	Kathryn Munsch	Maggie Johnson	Wesley Miller
Callie Harris	Katie & Kenny Tiffany	Nikki Vanden Heuvel	Wilhelmina Roberson
Carly Hulcher	Katie Attard	Pam Hahn	Yarenis & Ahlely Martinez
Char & Nick Hughes	Katie Mangus	Pamela Hahn	
Charlie, Isla & Grace DuMez	Kaylee Swift Wilson	Payton Danielle Clay	
Chris & Sarah Kleinjans	Kazmira Ruhland	Peter & Julie Mokma	
Christina Sherman	Kevin & Amy Rowland	R.J. Morales	
Courtney & Elisabeth	Kevin Geary & Steph Cosmas	Rachel Brennan	
Dan Kramer	Krista Fox & Ryan Walsh	Rachel D. Hachigian	
David Nelson	Laurel Boevé	Sarah Folino	
Debbie Diaz	Lauren & Kevin O'Neill	Stephanie Mathias	
Debbie Robbins	Lauren Gribeck	Steve & Courtney Chang	
Don & Vicki Harris	Lisa Miller	Susan & Scott Donegan	
Edward & Lynn Love	Lisa Notier	The Benoit Family	
Emily Bennett	Logan Stolt	The Cumiskey Family	
Erica Bergstrom	Lorrie, Terry, Quinton,	The Deckard Family	
Erin King	Caitryn, Savannah, Graesyn,	The Fedorov Family	
Gary & Lisa Murrell	& Paislee	The Harris Family	
Gary Hager	Marcel Rivera	The Klap Family	
Grandpa-cheese &	Marcia Rodeheffer	The Kragt Family	
Grammie Tanis	Mark Karlichek	The Lederhouse Family	
Greg & Geneva Karlichek	Marquia Bowen	The Macha Family	
Hannah Miller	Matthew Tabor	The Rankin-Clemments	

84533094R00027

Made in the USA
Lexington, KY
23 March 2018